POCKET IMAGES

Catholics in Cardiff

T0346943

John O'Sullivan, 2004.

POCKET IMAGES

Catholics in Cardiff

John O'Sullivan

NONSUCH

First published 2004
This new pocket edition 2007
Images unchanged from first edition

Nonsuch Publishing Limited
Cirencester Road, Chalford,
Stroud, Gloucestershire, GL6 8PE
www.nonsuch-publishing.com

Nonsuch Publishing is an imprint of NPI Media Group

British Library Cataloguing in Publication Data.
A catalogue record for this book is available from the British Library.

ISBN 978-1-84588-405-5

Typesetting and origination by Nonsuch Publishing Limited
Printed in Great Britain by Oaklands Book Services Limited

Contents

Acknowledgements

John O'Sullivan is grateful for the help given to him by: *Western Mail and Echo*; *St Peter's Chair* magazine; Bryn Jones and staff at Cardiff Central Library; Fr John Owen and Catholic People; Sisters of St Joseph of Annecy; Sisters of Nazareth; De La Salle Brothers; Beverley Carpanini, archbishop's secretary; Jim Carroll, Consul General for Ireland in Wales; Barry Tobin; John Sweeney; Joe Moore; Mary Sullivan; Vincent Doyle; Steve Doyle; Marion Qua.

About the Author

John O'Sullivan has been a journalist for fifty years and has worked for the *South Wales Echo*, *Western Mail*, *Daily Mail* and BBC Wales. He has also been writing for Catholic newspapers for forty-three years and took many of the photographs in this book himself. He left St Helen's school, in his home town of Barry, at the age of fourteen and is grateful to his family, his teachers and priests for helping him to understand and love his faith. This book would not have been possible without the support given by bishops, priests, nuns, brothers, lay people, fellow journalists and especially the photographers who recorded the various events and celebrations. God bless them all.

Introduction

Cardiff was little more than a village at the start of the nineteenth century, with its postal address listed as near Llantrisant, a market town twelve miles to the north.

By the end of the century, Cardiff was the biggest coal-exporting port in the world and was elevated to city status in 1905. Fifty years later it was declared the capital of Wales, and by the start of the twenty-first century the youngest capital in Europe was the home of the National Assembly, boasted one of the finest universities in Britain, and had been put on the world map in the fields of entertainment and sport, with the Millennium Stadium being acclaimed as one of the best sporting arenas in the world.

In 1820 there were only three Catholics in Cardiff—two Irishmen and a businessman from Usk. They used to walk to Merthyr or Newport to hear Mass before they persuaded Father Patrick Portal to travel from Merthyr to say the first post-reformation Mass in a private house, c.1822. By the start of the twenty-first century there were nineteen Catholic parishes, one university chaplaincy, seven convents, fourteen Catholic primary schools, four Catholic secondary schools and one Catholic independent school within the city boundaries. The archdiocese of Cardiff has its base in the city but also embraces the city of Newport and all the valley towns and parishes in the Vale of Glamorgan.

This book, compiled from my collection of photographs built up during the forty-three years I have been writing for Catholic newspapers, mainly illustrate Catholic life in the city of Cardiff, but some, regrettably not enough, reflects what has happened in other parts of the archdiocese.

Until the 1990s, the greatest annual event was the Corpus Christi (Body of Christ) celebrations, the first of which took place in the castle grounds in 1874, when the Third Marquis of Bute was one of the canopy bearers.

In the 1960s up to 10,000 children walked through the streets of Cardiff, wearing school uniforms or the dresses or suits that they had donned for their First Communion a few weeks earlier. The boys and girls who walked through the crowd-lined streets in the sixties are now middle-aged and will enjoy sharing those happy days with their children and grandchildren. 'Is that really you, Bampa, in short trousers and wearing a cap that looked too big for you? Have you still got that lovely white dress, Nana?'

There are school photographs, including one of St David's Junior School, which dates back to the nineteenth century when the class furniture included a magnificent rocking horse. Events at the Cathedral and stately occasions when archbishops or bishops were involved, give a small insight into church life. Many parishioners will recognise the priests, many of whom are now dead.

Former pupils of St Cadoc's, Llanrumney, will be reminded of the 1968 visit to the school by Mother Teresa. The gallery of photographs of nuns gives only a brief glimpse of those devoted women who have given valiant service to education, nursing and social work in the area. You will have the opportunity to relive pilgrimages to Lourdes, Cardigan and Penrhys, and there are interesting groups of lay people which may stir memories.

The greatest day in the history of the Catholic Church in Wales was 2 June 1982—the day that Pope John Paul II presided over a concelebrated Mass for 150,000 people at Pontcanna Fields, Cardiff. It was the day that the Holy Father was made a freeman of Cardiff, an honour he shares with Winston Churchill, Viscount George Thomas, former prime minister Jim Callaghan, Nelson Mandela and many other great people.

On his last afternoon in Britain, the Pope led a celebration for young people at Ninian Park, the home of Cardiff City Football Club. It was his last engagement in Britain and he returned to Rome from Cardiff Wales Airport.

It was another twenty years before another great man from the Vatican visited Cardiff. Cardinal Francis Arinze, President of the Pontifical Council for Inter Religious Dialogue, came at the invitation of Father John Owen, Chaplain to Cardiff University. Cardinal Arinze, from Nigeria, has been named as one of the possible successors to Pope John Paul II. In Cardiff he called for universities in Britain to introduce courses where people of all faiths can study each other's beliefs so there will be greater understanding between the various sects. It was a timely appeal, made just four months after terrorists destroyed the Twin Towers in New York, killing more than 3,000 people. My prayer is that Cardinal Arinze's idea is taken on board by universities, not only in Britain but throughout the troubled world.

In 1999, the Wales Famine Forum, under the chairmanship of John Sweeney established a memorial at Cathays cemetery, Cardiff, to the Great Irish Famine of the 1840s. It is fitting that this should be in Cardiff, where thousands of refugees from the potato famine settled in the mid-nineteenth century.

As the Church faced the challenge of the new Millennium, there were dark clouds over the archdiocese, but the problems which sadly led to two priests being sent to prison should not mar the glorious history of Catholicism in this corner of the world. These photographs are a reminder that the faith of our fathers has always been strong and can stay strong in Wales, especially in Cardiff, which the late Bishop Langton Fox, of Menevia, described at the time of the Pope's visit as the most Catholic city in Britain.

There are few photographs of buildings in the book but two images at the end illustrate how the architecture of the inside of churches has changed over 150 years. One of the scenes has a family link to two Irishmen who were hanged following the Easter Rising in 1916.

It has been a privilege for me to have reported on so many Catholic events since my debut covering Archbishop Michael McGrath in 1961.

John O'Sullivan
June 2004

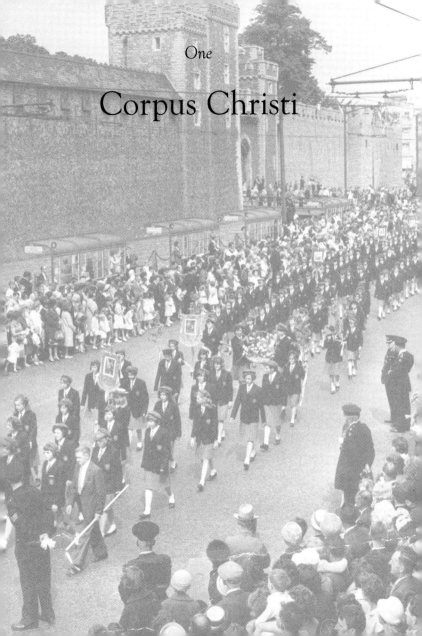

One

Corpus Christi

Above: This artist's impression of a Corpus Christi celebration held at Cardiff Castle in 1891 was published in the magazine *St Peter's Chair*, which can be seen at the city's Central Library. Amongst others, it shows Father McClement, Monsignor Williams, Father Matthews and Father J.B. Moore.

Opposite above: This postcard of a Corpus Christi procession in the grounds of Cardiff Castle was posted from Pontypridd to a Mrs H. Case at No. 5 Maughan Terrace, Penarth, in 1904.

Opposite below: An early photograph of a Corpus Christi procession outside Cardiff Castle in 1911.

Above: Girls from St David's School pose for the camera in their First Communion dresses in 1962. Archbishop John Murphy (back row, centre) is flanked by Father Sam McCurdy and Father Bernard Cosulich. Headteacher Con Collins is on the left.

Left: St Patrick's Pipe Band in 1925. (Courtesy of Michael Flynn)

Opposite above: St Patrick's Pipe Band in 1962. (Courtesy of Michael Flynn)

Opposite below: St David's boys on parade.

Opposite above: Pupils from St Joseph's Convent School in 1962.

Opposite below: De La Salle boys pose for the camera in the castle grounds in 1962.

Right: Lady Mary School arrive at Cardiff Castle during a Corpus Christi procession in 1964.

Below: Pupils from St Cadoc's Infant School.

Left: Corpus Christi procession outside Cardiff Castle. A stream of white dresses in a crowd-lined street.

Below: St David's Cathedral choir.

Opposite above: Blessed Sacrament procession, 1964.

Opposite below: Monsignor Peter Gavin, Vicar General and Parish Priest of Penarth, blesses the crowd at the Corpus Christi held at Cardiff Castle in 1964.

Above: Pupils from St Joseph's Junior School, seen here in the 1960s.

Right: Flower girls, teachers and classmates from St Joseph's Infant School.

Opposite above: More pupils from St Cadoc's, Llanrumney, 1964.

Opposite below: A sea of faces at the Corpus Christi celebrations, 1964.

Girls from
St Cadoc's
Junior School
enjoying the
1964 event.

The junior girls from St Alban's School, Splott.

Smart boys of St Joseph's Junior School march past the photographer.

Girls from St Peter's Infant School smile for the camera in their First Communion dresses.

St David's infants and juniors take part in a Corpus Christi procession.

Classmates from St Alban's Infant School.

Contingent from St Patrick's School, Grangetown.

St David's infants are escorted by their teachers along the High Street during a Corpus Christi procession.

St Joseph's infants. Overlooking the procession is the statue of John, the second Marquis of Bute, sculpted by I. Evan Thomas in the mid-nineteenth century.

Boys from Bishop Mostyn School, Ely, line up in 1964. The school was later renamed Immaculate Heart of Mary.

St Joseph's Convent School, 1964. The teacher wearing the hat is Carol Hunt.

Sister Terisita escorts pupils from St Joseph's Convent School on a Corpus Christi procession through the city centre.

St David's boys pose for the photograph in the school playground.

Lady Mary boys in 1964.

Above left: In the 1980s the Corpus Christi celebrations were held at the Arms Park rugby ground. The man in the centre in an open-neck shirt was Tom German, a parishioner of St Peter's church.

Above right: John Williams, leader of St Alban's Band, leading community singing at the Arms Park.

St Alban's Band playing at Arms Park in 1984.

Folk singer and broadcaster Frank Hennessy is seen here entertaining the Arms Park crowd at the Corpus Christi event in 1984.

Howard Green, managing director of the *Western Mail and Echo* newspaper receives Holy Communion from Archbishop John Ward at Arms Park in 1983. Waiting is Howard's wife, Audrey.

Following the Pope's visit to Cardiff in 1982, seven men were made papal knights at a Corpus Christi celebration. From left to right: architect Tom Price, restaurant owner Eddie Rabaiotti, Sir James Lyons (who was made a papal knight before the Pope's visit), managing director of the *Western Mail and Echo* Howard Green, Colonel John O'Brien, accountant David Hirst, Chief Constable Sir John Woodcock and Assistant Chief Constable Viv Brooks.

The crowd join in the singing at Arms Park, *c.*1984.

In 1993 the Corpus Christi celebrations were transferred to the Cardiff International Arena.

Part of the congregation at the 1993 celebrations.

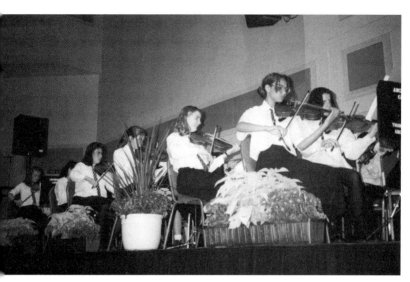

Music for the 1993 celebration was provided by a school orchestra.

Time to adjust a head-dress while waiting for the 1993 service to start.

Above left: In procession at the Cardiff International Arena.

Above right: Two friends from St Alban's parish.

Archbishop John Ward is seen here distributing Holy Communion to children at the Cardiff International Arena.

The traditional Corpus Christi processions came to an end in the 1990s, although the feast is still marked in parishes and deaneries. These children took part in a celebration held at Nazareth House in 2001.

Priests and nuns in procession at Nazareth House in 2001.

Children walking in the Corpus Christi procession in 2001.

Part of the crowd watching the 2001 event.

Opposite above: Bishop Edwin Regan of Wrexham chatting to youngsters after the service.

Opposite middle: Bishop Regan celebrated Benediction in 2001.

Opposite below: Children join Bishop Regan for a photograph.

All set for the procession.

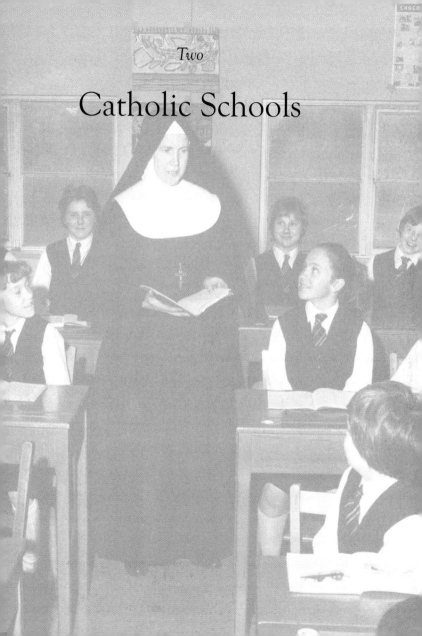

Two

Catholic Schools

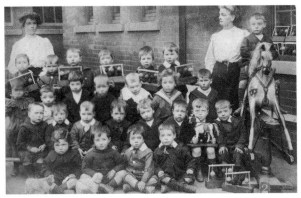

An early class photograph from St David's School, Cardiff, in the nineteenth century.

Christmas party at St Teilo's, Whitchurch, in 1947.

Girls from St Joseph's Convent School are pictured ready for P.E. in the 1950s.

St Jospeh's Convent, class photograph in June 1950.

Another St Joseph's Convent School class.

St Joseph's Convent pupils in December 1948.

A reunion of former pupils of St Joseph's Convent School, held in the 1960s.

Right: Sister Cyril oversees a school play, shortly before her retirement as head of St Joseph's Primary School, Cardiff.

Below: Two Sisters from St Joseph of Annecy are pictured here with a First Communion Class at St Teilo's, Whitchurch, in the early 1970s.

Canon Patrick Creed with First Communion class, St Teilo's, Whitchurch, in 1972.

Sister Vincent with pupils at St Joseph's Convent School in 1963.

Monsignor Gerald Chidgey, chairman of the governors of Bishop Hannon School, Cardiff, is seen here presenting a cheque for £400 to Joe Daley, trustee for the Handicapped Children's Pilgrimage Trust, in 1977. The money, raised from the proceeds of the school bazaar and other activities, was collected by pupils of Bishop Hannon School to enable the trust to send five youngsters on a pilgrimage to Lourdes.

St Patrick's School, Grangetown, at the unveiling of the Wales Famine Memorial at Cathay's cemetery on 17 March 1999.

American writer and broadcaster Bishop Fulton Sheen with pupils at Newport in 1971.
(Courtesy of O'Sullivan Archives)

St Teilo's children's choir in 2001.

Senior boys from St Helen's School, Barry, in the late 1940s.

Canon William Boulton making a presentation to Father Michael Murphy, St Helen's School, Barry, in the 1950s. Headmaster John Kelly is on the left.

John Rowley's (seated, centre) class at St Helen's School, Barry, in the 1950s.

Archbishop John Murphy admires a model of ship at St Cadoc's School (later renamed St Richard Gwyn), Barry, in the 1960s. The headmaster, Ernest Brooks, is standing second from the left.

Fifty years on: a reunion of old boys from St Helen's School. From left to right: Micky Murphy, former schoolboy heavyweight champion of Britain, Arthur Cheek, Jimmy Hurley and Denis (Dan) McCarthy.

John Kanu, a refugee from war-torn Sierra Leone, visiting St Francis School, Ely, Cardiff, in 2002.

The Immaculate Heart of Mary Band from Haverfordwest regularly played at Catholic events. They are seen here at a national pilgrimage to Cardigan.

The cast of the Nativity play at St Teilo's in 2002.

Three

Catholic Cathedral

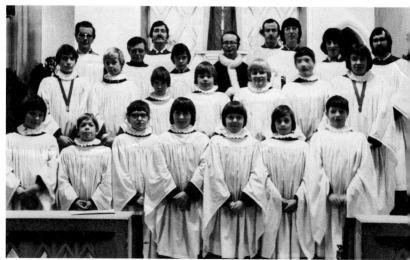

Archbishop John Murphy talking to Brother Alfred and De La Salle boys who made up the cathedral choir in the 1960s. Father Bernard Cosulich is at the back.

Opposite above: Altar boys at St David's Cathedral, Cardiff, with Father Sean Kearney. Second from left in the second row is Terry Holmes, who went on to play rugby for Wales. (Photograph courtesy of John Adams, pictured far right, back row)

Opposite below: St David's Cathedral choir, with the future Bishop Edwin Regan of Wrexham, in the 1970s.

A group photograph of St David's choir before setting off to Rome in 1968. Seated in the middle of the front row is Alan Rees, who later became Abbot of Belmont.

Opposite above: Brother Alfred, Archbishop John Murphy and Father Bernard Cosulich with the cathedral choir in the 1960s. (Courtesy *South Wales Echo*)

Opposite below: The cathedral choir in the 1960s, with conductor and organist David Neville on the far left. (Courtesy *South Wales Echo*)

Priests using the non-conformist church in Charles Street, Cardiff, as a vesting room for a Maundy Thursday ceremony at St David's Cathedral in the late 1990s.

The scene inside St David's Cathedral at Archbishop Murphy's Jubilee Mass in the 1980s. (Courtesy *South Wales Echo*)

Four

Bishops

Above left: Bishop Thomas Brown, appointed to Wales and Herefordshire in 1840, was buried at Belmont Abbey after his death in 1880.

Above right: Bishop Francis Vaughan, who left St Helen's, Barry, in 1925 to become Bishop of Menevia at Wrexham.

Left: Revd Francis Mostyn who was Archbishop of Cardiff from 1921 to 1939.

Opposite above: The funeral of Archbishop Michael McGrath at Llantarnam Abbey in 1961. He had been Archbishop of Cardiff from 1940. Bishop John Petit, of Menevia, conducted the service.

Archbishop John Murphy is seen here on his way to St David's Cathedral for his enthronement on 31 October 1961. He retired as Archbishop of Cardiff in 1983 and died in 1995.

Archbishop John Murphy being greeted by his secretary, Father Daniel Mullins, on his return from the Vatican Council in 1962. In 1985 Father Mullins became Bishop of Menevia.

Right: Former Catholic Lord Mayor of Cardiff, Sir James Lyons, with Archbishop Murphy and Bishop Petit at Cardiff–Wales Airport when the bishops were on their way to Lourdes.

Opposite above: Canon Robert Reardon, Vicar General in 2004, being ordained by Archbishop John Murphy in 1971. Father Ambrose Walsh is assisting.

Opposite below: Archbishop John Murphy on a visit to Maesteg in 1963. Assisting is Father Sam McCurdy, who died in 1970.

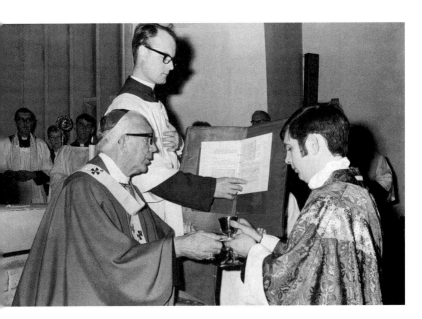

59

Left: Archbishop John Murphy ordained Father Maurice Gallagher at St Alban's church, Cardiff, in 1965. Father Maurice was later killed in a road accident in Africa.

Below: Cardinal John Heenan visited the Cardiff archdiocese in 1967. He and Archbishop Murphy are seen here being greeted by Father John Forbes at St Joseph's School, Swansea.

Cardinal Heenan and Archbishop Murphy with Welsh author and broadcaster Saunders Lewis, a parishioner of St Joseph's church, Penarth.

The late Canon Tom Dunne with Archbishop Murphy at St Brigid's church, Cardiff.

Above: Archbishop Murphy helping his former diocese of Shrewsbury to celebrate winning the Catenian Clergy Golf Trophy at Newman College, Birmingham, in 1971. The trophy had been presented to the Shrewsbury team—winners of the Universe Clergy Golf Tournament.

Left: Three former Bishops of Menevia. From left to right: Langton Fox, John Ward and James Hannigan.

Opposite: Archbishop Murphy with Father Gerald Mahon (left), Superior General of the Mill Hill Missionaries, at the centenary celebrations at Courtfield, Herefordshire, the family home of Cardinal Herbert Vaughan.

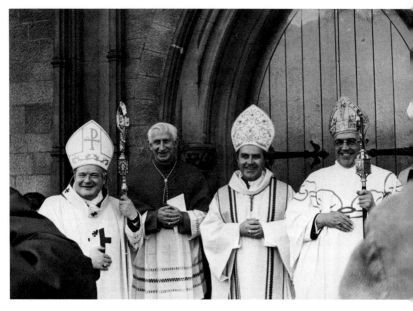

Above: Bishop James Hannigan (right) was ordained Bishop of Menevia in 1983 and died as Bishop of Wrexham in 1994. Pictured with him, from left to right, are Archbishop John Ward, Cardinal John Hume and the Bishop of Donegal.

Left: Bishop Daniel Mullins at St Joseph's Cathedral, Swansea, after being enthroned as Bishop of Menevia in 1985.

Opposite above: The scene inside St Joseph's Cathedral when the diocese of Menevia was transferred from Wrexham in 1985. The Apostolic Mandate for Menevia was read by Canon Clyde Johnson. For seventy-one years, Rome had administered Wales from Cardiff and Wrexham, but in 1985 the Pope approved plans to create a third centre at Swansea. This reflected the growing need for the Church to be closer to its growing flock, said to be expanding at the rate of 400 people a year.

Caldy Island is in the Menevia Diocese and Prince Charles visited the Cistercian Community there.

Left: Archbishop Peter Smith at a press conference after being appointed Archbishop of Cardiff in 2001. With him is his Vicar General, Canon Robert Reardon.

Below: Archbishop Peter Smith greets people after his enthronement at St David's Cathedral, Cardiff, in 2001.

A warm welcome for Archbishop Smith from Madeline Walters, chair of St Teilo's Parish Council.

Greeting a new Archbishop.

Above: Archbishop Smith has a word with Nigerian priest Father Kevin, who was a student at the university in Cardiff.

Left: Archbishop Dilwyn Lewis was a foundling who was left on the doorstep of a Bridgend orphanage when he was only a few days old. A convert to Catholicism, he was appointed by Pope John Paul II as administrator of the St Mary Major Basilica in Rome.

Opposite above: When Bishop Dilwyn Lewis visited Usk, these pilgrims joined him on a walk to the grave of St David Lewis.

Opposite below left: Egyptian-born Mark Jabale, formerly Abbot of Belmont, succeeded Bishop Mullins as Bishop of Menevia in 2000.

Opposite below right: Alwyn Rice Jones, Anglican Archbishop of Wales, congratulates Bishop Edwin Regan on his ordination as Bishop of Wrexham in 1994.

Cardinal Glemp, of Poland, on a visit to Cardiff in the 1970s.

The apostolic delegate Archbishop Barbaroti with St Alban's band leader John Williams in the 1970s.

Five

Catholic Priests and Brothers

Left: This time-worn photograph shows priests heading for St David's Cathedral in the 1960s, headed by Father James McNiff, who died in 1965, and Father Francis Poyner, who died in 1986.

Below: Priests at All Hallows, Miskin, in the 1990s.

Above: Father Donal Gillespie, parish priest of Kenfig Hill, was the first priest on the scene following the bomb blast in his home town of Omagh, Northern Ireland, on Sunday 15 August 1998, which resulted in twenty-nine deaths and many more injuries.

Right: Canon Tom Phelan was parish priest of St Patrick's, Grangetown, Cardiff, for more than forty years.

Canon Tom Phelan with parishioners in 1969.

Maesteg-born Father John Rohan, who died in 1994 whilst he was parish priest of Merthyr. His own father had died in a pit accident.

Father Chris Delaney (OSB) led a cycling party from St Mary's, Canton, Cardiff, on a pilgrimage to Lourdes in the 1960s.

Canon Patrick Creed, who was parish priest of St Teilo's, Whitchurch, Cardiff, for forty-three years.

Above: Father Peter Collins (left) with Father Bernard Whitehouse, whom he succeeded when he became Dean of St David's Cathedral in 2001.

Above: Father Frank Mulvey, the parish priest of the Blessed Sacrament, Rumney, Cardiff, putting at Radyr Golf Club and watched by fellow priests.

Right: Father Frank Mulvey (left) and Father Phillip McAuliffe entertaining at a St Patrick's Day social. Father McAuliffe died in 1994.

Opposite below: Father John Doman is a former Sikh, who served as a Rosminian priest in both Cardiff and India. He is seen here, third from the left of the men at the top of the picture, on a picnic with his family in the Rosminian House in Guildford.

Father Bernard Whitehouse, chaplain, has a word with Lord Mayor Ricky Ormonde and his wife, Lady Mayoress Valerie in 1995.

Group Captain Gerard Monaghan, chaplain of RAF St Athan, teasing a horse near the camp in the 1960s. Father Gerard, who died in 1989, later became parish priest of St Cuthbert's, Cardiff and Abertillery.

Father David Myers, rector, with the Dowager Lady of Bute, inaugurating the new bells at St Peter's church, Cardiff.

Father Phillip McAuliffe with fellow Corkman Father Finbarr O'Leary, who left Cardiff to serve in South American Missions.

Left: Cardiff-born Father Christopher Hancock was ordained by Archbishop Peter Smith as a Mill Hill priest at St Mary and All Angels church, Cardiff, on 19 June 2004. He will serve in Cameroon.

Below: Father Christopher Hancock celebrating his first Mass at St Mary and All Angels church, Cardiff, on 20 June 2004.

Newly ordained Father Christopher Hancock blessing Canon John Maguire, Parish Priest of St Mary and All Angels.

Archbishop John Ward with Canon John McLoughlin, Parish Priest of Sacred Heart, Leckwith, who died in 1998.

These are some of the many priests who were educated at St Illtyd's College, Cardiff. Third from left in the front row is Monsignor Gerald Chidgey.

St Illtyd's College was founded by the De La Salle Brothers in 1922, When the order left Cardiff in the 1990s, there was a big hand for the doyen of teachers, Brother Luke, second from right.

De La Salle Brothers at a thank-you Mass at St Alban's, Cardiff, in the 1990s.

Rugby international David Bishop with Brother Cyril, one of his former teachers. A Pontypool and Wales scrum half, David played rugby league for Wales in the 1980s and went on to become player-coach of Pontypool. He played a leading role in saving the club from relegation to Division Two in the late 1990s.

Brother Terrence distributing Communion at St Illtyd's College Mass, in 1976.

Gathered to celebrate Golden Jubilee of St Illtyd's College in 1972. From left to right: Brother Alexander; Archbishop Murphy; Sir Charles Hallinan; future Speaker George Thomas, MP; future prime minister James Callaghan MP; Brother Victor and Bishop Mullins.

Six

Catholic Nuns and Priests

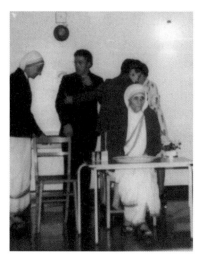

Above left: World-famous Mother Teresa at St Cadoc's School, Llanrumney, Cardiff, in 1968. The school had collected enough money for her to buy an ambulance.

Above right: The Poor Clares of Hereford during midday Prayer of the Church in 1993.

Above: Old and new: in the 1960s the Sisters of Charity of St Vincent de Paul changed their mode of dress from that worn by Sister Cecilia (centre) to that worn by Sister Catherine and Sister Bernadette at their convent in Cathedral Road, Cardiff.

Opposite below: Some Poor Clare Sisters. From left to right are Sisters Bonaventure, Mary Francis and Leonard, packing the altar bread at their convent in Hereford.

The Sisters of St Joseph of Annecy in procession at Llantarnam Abbey in the 1960s.

The clothing ceremony of new nuns at Llantarnam Abbey in the 1960s.

Sisters Josephine and Veronica, former midwives at St Joseph's Nursing Home, Malpas, with some of the parents whose babies they delivered.

Sisters of St Joseph of Annecy who have worked as teachers, nurses and social workers in the Cardiff archdiocese.

Sisters from Nazareth House heading for a polling booth in Colum Place, Cardiff, in 1974.

Celebrating at Nazareth House when Joan Thomas (sitting front right) was awarded a Beni Merenti Medal in 2002. Joan was a child at Nazareth House and returned to live there in her later years.

Poor Clare Sisters joined Archbishop John Ward for his Golden Jubilee celebrations in the 1990s.

Sister Veronica and Sister Dominic Savio stayed at St Clare's Convent in Porthcawl after fleeing the civil war in Kosovo.

The Sisters of Charity ran a hostel for students at Nos 41–43 Cathedral Road in the 1960s.

Above left: Sister Patricia Maxwell, of the Sisters of Charity, pictured here at Roath Park, Cardiff, after fleeing the civil war in Sierra Leone.

Above right: Sister Denise Gardiner, of the Sisters of Charity, is pictured here with Caldy, the collie cross, her hearing-dog for the deaf, at her convent home in Talbot Street, Cardiff, in the 1990s.

Above left: Mother M. Finbarr Quinn was headmistress at St Joseph's Convent School, Cardiff, in the 1950s and later held senior posts among the Sisters of St Joseph of Annecy at Llantarnam Abbey. She died on 11 November 1985, aged sixty-six years.

Above right: The much-loved Mother Felicitas, a native of Penarth, who was head teacher of St Joseph's Primary School, Cardiff, for many years.

Left: Sister Anne Bernadette, of the Sisters of St Joseph of Annecy.

Sister Monica of Llantarnam Abbey, who was elected Mother General of the Sisters of St Joseph of Annecy, being interviewed by John O'Sullivan.

Sister Justina, Matron Superior of St Winifred's Hospital, shares a joke with Speaker of the Commons George Thomas and Sir Julian Hodge in the Sir Julian Hodge Wing.

Missionary Sisters of Mary, who served in the Dowlais parish.

Above left: Home from the African Missions, Sister Mary Andrew Kydd, of the Sisters of Charity, with her mother outside St Teilo's church.

Above right: Sister John Joseph, of the Sacred Heart of Jesus and Mary Order, enjoying an ice cream on the beach at Margate during a break from the Lord Ninian Hospital, Cardiff.

On their way to Lourdes in the 1960s. Morine Harford stands second from the left in Welsh costume. She returned to visit the shrine in France more than twenty times after being cured of throat cancer while on a visit there.

Oposite below: Situated on the road between Newport and Pontypool is the imposing Llantarnam Abbey, the Provincial House of the Sisters of St Joseph of Annecy.

Overleaf: The Welsh National Pilgrimage at Lourdes in 1989.

Left: Archbishop John Murphy stops to share a joke with Maurice Handford on his way to Lourdes in 1967. A total of 280 pilgrims went on the eighth Welsh National Pilgrimage. They left Cardiff Airport in three plane-loads. Archbishop Murphy was accompanied by Bishop Petit of Menevia and Bishop Fox, Auxiliary in Menevia.

Below left: Maurice Hanford was bedridden from birth but this did not prevent him from going on pilgrimages to Lourdes and Rome. He is seen here with one of his helpers, Vincent Doyle, and Rosemary Kelly (right).

Below right: Michael O'Sullivan, of Dowlais, with Rosary beads and bubblegum at Penrhys. Michael died of leukaemia at the age of twelve.

Opposite above: Knights of St Columba carrying the statue of Our Lady of the Taper at the National Welsh shrine at Cardigan, May 1984.

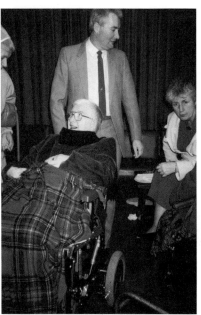

Bishop Langton Fox (centre) after the National Eisteddfod Mass—Offeren Eisteddfod Aberteifi—at Cardigan in August 1976. Canon Seamus Cunnane, Father John Fitzgerald and the poet Raymond Garlick (signing books) are also in the picture. On the right are Patrick and Carys Whelan and their children. Carys later became the first woman president of the ecumenical group Cytun.

Pilgrims at the shrine of Our Lady of Penrhys in the Rhondda.

Father Tony Hodges signing to deaf children in St Mary's Parish, Cardiff.

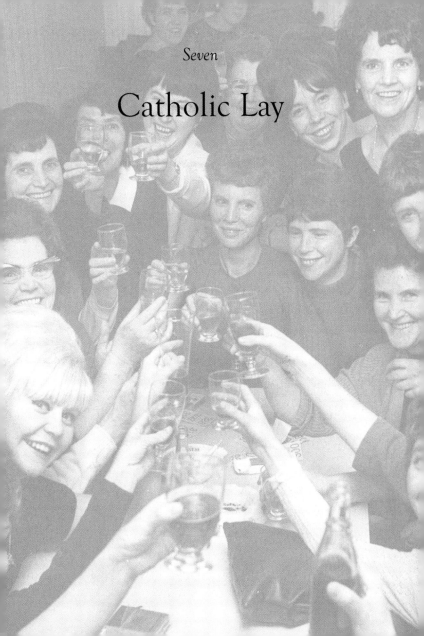

Seven

Catholic Lay

Above: Anthony Packer, Lithuanian Consul to Wales (centre) with Tom McGary, former president of the National Union of Students in Wales, and University Chaplain Father John Owen.

Right: Father Leo Ceaser (OSB) on his retirement as chaplain of Cardiff University in the 1970s.

Opposite above: Father Sean Kearney with St Vincent de Paul Society members, Cardiff, in 1969. The St Vincent de Paul Society (SVP) is an international Christian organisation. Although Catholic in origin and character, it is dedicated to helping anyone in need.

Opposite below: A Golden Wedding anniversary celebration was held for retired teachers William and Elizabeth Wall at the Cardiff University Chaplaincy, where their son Father Brian Wall, was chaplain.

Students at Mass at the University chaplaincy in Cardiff in 2004.

Marion Qua Li Lian with her family after graduating with her master's degree in Law at Cardiff University in the year 2000. Marion, who later qualified as an advocate and solicitor in Kuala Lumpur, played an active part in Catholic circles in Cardiff. She is of Irish descent on the side of her mother, Margaret, whose grandmother's name was McIntyre.

Papal knight and charitable founder of the Bank of Wales, Sir Julian Hodge, pictured with his family after being knighted by the Queen at Buckingham Palace in 1970. Sir Julian died aged ninety-nine in 2004.

Canon Francis Poyner and members of the Legion of Mary at a farewell dinner held for Terry and Sybil Chidgey when they left Cardiff for Birmingham in the 1960s. (Courtesy of Lew Yapp)

Above: Boxer 'Peerless' Jim Driscoll (seated on chair, centre) and his wife, Edith (seated on chair next to him, left) with guests at a wedding in Newtown, Cardiff, in Edwardian days. Born in 1880 in the part of the area then known as Newtown, or Cardiff's Little Ireland, Jim Driscoll gave up the chance of fighting for the featherweight championship of the world to keep a promise to take part in an exhibition bout at the Park Hall in Cardiff in aid of his favourite charity, the Assault at Arms Committee, which supported Nazareth House. A great supporter of his church and community, he became respected across the world for his skill as a boxer. After his death in 1925, Jim was buried at Cathay's cemetery and thousands of people lined the streets to watch the funeral procession. Outside Cardiff Castle the coffin was placed on a gun carriage and an army band played solemn music as members of the Second Battalion of the Welch Regiment paid their tribute. The headstone was paid for by the Sisters of Nazareth. In 1997 a statue of Peerless Jim was erected near the site of the former Central Boys' Club where he used to train.

Left: The women of Newtown marked the demolition of Cardiff's Little Ireland in the mid-1960s with a traditional Irish wake.

Choir at St Teilo's Whitchurch, Cardiff, at the opening of the church on 18 June 1964.

Altar boys at St Teilo's Whitchurch, Cardiff, at the opening of the church on 18 June 1964.

Above left: Billy O'Neill, of St Peter's parish, was still collecting for charity in his nineties.

Above right: Andrea and Dominic Franchie, parishioners of St Teilo's, were happily married for nearly seventy years.

Above left: Altar boy Michael Martin found a new way to transport programmes during a pilgrimage to Cardigan.

Above right: Albert Bridle, an outstanding Catholic youth leader in Cardiff, organised Christmas Day lunches for lonely and homeless people for more than thirty years. He died in 1985.

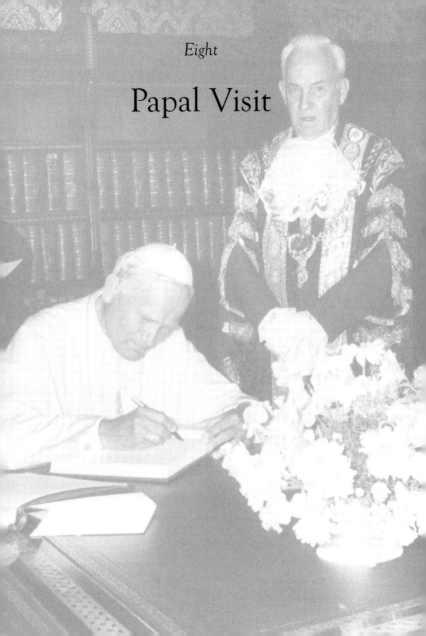

Eight

Papal Visit

Pope John Paul II blesses the crowd at Pontcanna Fields, Cardiff, on 2 June 1982.

Vast crowds turned out to greet the Holy Father in Cardiff in 1982.

Left: A special message for the Holy Father. The Pontcanna crowd encompassed a diverse age range, including students and pensioners.

Below: A fold in the poster suggests it might have been a bottle of pop they were greeting!

Opposite above: Sisters of St Joseph of Annecy at the Papal Mass at Pontcanna Fields.

Opposite below: Sisters of the Sacred Heart of Jesus and Mary were among the 150,000 people who attended the Papal Mass.

Three smiling Sisters from Nazareth House enjoying a cup of tea while waiting at Pontcanna for the Pope to arrive. From left to right are Angel Raphael, Mother St Mel and Sister Louise.

A happy group of youngsters from St Cuthbert's parish, the Docks, Cardiff. From left to right are Zoe Hassan, aged fifteen, Baindu Foday, aged five, Anne Marie Foday, aged thirteen, and Nancy Foday, aged twelve.

More than 150,000 people attended the Papal Mass at Pontcanna Fields. The Pope sat on a specially designed dais at the start of the last open-air Mass of his six-day visit to Britain, where he greeted the people of Wales in their own language.

Some of the 5,000 volunteers who were stewards at the Papal Mass.

Above: Old friends: Polish-born Pope John Paul II with Father Edward Rytko, who was chaplain to the Polish community in South Wales for decades. As trainee priests, the two men were fellow students in Rome.

Left: The Holy Father was made a Freeman of the City of Cardiff, watched by the Lord Mayor, Councillor Philip Dunleavy.

Opposite above: Mary and Kenneth Camilleri met the Holy Father in Rome.

Opposite below: The Pope-mobile, which the Holy Father used while in Cardiff. It was later bought by Cardiff businessman John Davies, of Davies Colour Photographers.

Left: In 2002 Cardinal Francis Arinze, President of the Pontifical Council for Inter-Religious Dialogue at the Vatican, visited Cardiff and was presented with a miner's lamp.

Below: Cardinal Arinze talking to students after celebrating Mass at the University Chaplaincy.

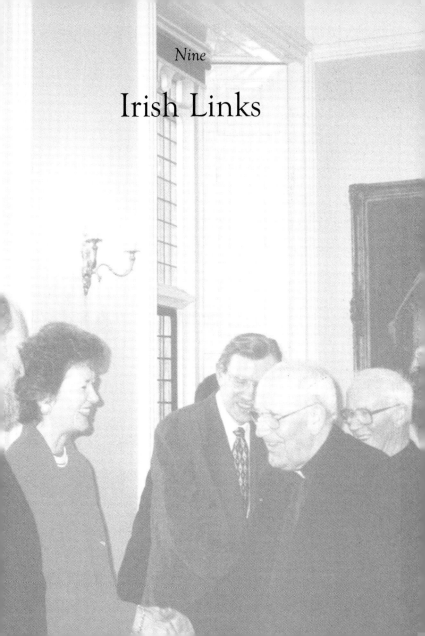

Nine

Irish Links

Ireland's president Mary Robinson with guests at a reception at Cardiff Castle.

Ireland's president Mary Robinson greeting Canon Patrick Daley, Father John Fahy and Father Liam Shore at Cardiff Castle.

President Robinson's successor Mary Macaleese also visited Cardiff and is seen with the Consul General for Ireland in Wales, Jim Carroll (right). Mary Sullivan, chairman of the Newtown Association, and her husband Vincent enjoyed the occasion.

President Macaleese and Jim Carroll with eminent Welsh writer and psychiatrist Harri Pritchard Jones.

Above: Ireland's Foreign Secretary, David Andrew (right) in Cardiff.

Left: The National Memorial to the victims of the Great Irish Famine of the 1840s was erected in Cathay's cemetery in 1999 by the Wales Famine Forum. The Irish Famine of 1846–50 took as many as one million lives from hunger and disease.

Opposite above: Part of the crowd at a ceremony at the National Famine Memorial.

Ireland's ambassador Ted Barrington (fourth from left) led the Famine Walk in Cardiff in 2000.

A few yards from the National Famine Memorial is this monument which marks the graves of Bishop Cuthbert Hedley and Archbishop Francis Mostyn.

St Peter's church, Cardiff, prior to the Second Vatican Council. One of the craftsmen who created the magnificent screen was the father of Irish patriots Padraig and Willy Pearse, who were both hanged in Dublin after the Easter Uprising in 1916.